Take a Deep Breath

Denise Blake

SUMMER PALACE PRESS

First published in 2004 by

Summer Palace Press
Cladnageeragh, Kilbeg, Kilcar, County Donegal, Ireland

in association with
Donegal County Council
Readers and Writers Programme

Printed by Nicholson & Bass Ltd.

A catalogue record for this book is available
from the British Library

ISBN   0   9544752   8   3

This book is printed on elemental chlorine-free paper

for
Laurence
and for
Damien, Aiden and Ian

Acknowledgments

Some of the poems in this book have previously appeared in: *Beyond the Rubicon* (Covehill Press 1999); *Poetry Ireland Review* (Issues 65, 66, 68, 70 and 76); *The SHOp* (Issues 8, 12 and 14); *The Stinging Fly* (Issues 11, 14 and 18); *Women's Work* (VII and X); *Black Mountain Review* (Issues 7 and 9) and *A Deeper Light*.

Some poems were recorded on Errigal Writers' CD – *Eleven Ways to Kiss the Ground.*

Biographical Note

Denise Blake was born in Ohio, USA in 1958 and came to Letterkenny, County Donegal in 1969. She was shortlisted for the *Sunday Tribune/Hennessy Awards* for first short story in 1994, was winner of the Donegal short story award at the Allingham Competition, was broadcast on *Sunday Miscellany*, RTE, and a dramatic piece, *Grandmother's Nights*, was performed in the Balor Theatre, Ballybofey. She won the Charles Macklin Award for poetry in 1999 and was a prize-winner in the Boyle Festival 2003. In that year she read as part of Poetry Ireland Introductions, at the Errigal Arts Festival and at the Samhain Festival, Gortahork. She is a founder member of the Errigal Writers' Group and received an MA in poetry from Lancaster University through the Poets' House, Falcarragh, County Donegal. She has facilitated writing groups and has translated into English the Irish poet Cathal Ó Searcaigh.

CONTENTS

The Leaving

Totem-poles stand guard.
We sit like squaws around a camp-fire.
Marshmallows roast on sticks and graham
cracker smores melt in aluminum foil.
Our Guide plays the guitar
while my best friend sings *Kumbaya*.
There are flashes of fairy lights
as fireflies move around us.

My last night at Camp Christopher, Ohio.
My last week living in the States.
A waterfall is building up inside.
In a few days I will be flying to Donegal,
after years of dancing self-taught jigs
in our den, or playing the record,
How are things in Glocca Morra?

At the camp-fire we are given small logs
like baby canoes to hold a candle.
We carry them in procession to the river
where the Guide lights one at a time.
Don't cry kid, she says, *you'll be back.*
I kneel down to place my offering,
as a hundred flames float away.

Letterkenny 567

The black phone didn't have a dial,
just a small side-handle to crank.
Number please?
Letterkenny 32.
The operator might say, *No point ringing there,*
they are all away for the day.
If you did get through there was a tick-tick
like a cricket in a night-forest.
Someone was listening.

Words came at me in swarms of locusts.
Chips were crisps. French fries were chips.
Jelly was jam. Jello was jelly.
No one knew what pizza was.
It wasn't only pizza we had left behind,
but clothes in psychedelic patterns.
There, I had worn the phone as an earring
while having endless talks full of baloney.

They didn't have baloney here, but Spam;
apple-pie sweets and gobstoppers.
I needed a lot of those.
Never asked the right questions:
Where does your Father work?
Never gave the right answers:
Yes. I do miss Cleveland.

You couldn't just ring Cleveland.
Calls were as sacred as Our Lady.
Neighbours came to our house
for urgent messages, left coins beside the phone.
And when I did make a local call,
Don't talk too long.
You're not in America now.

The Piggeries

Two sheds like upturned boats moulded
from layers of hemp sacks and cement.
Grandad carried me there, to watch them
sleep. Sows lay with their piglets
tucked in around them as under a blanket.

Cousins, we all played in the yard,
grouping in gangs and regrouping
for red light, green light; boys against
the girls; tip rugby; block one two three.

When the men stomped their feet, banged
sticks against the ground, we scattered.
I cowered on the edge as they shouted,
drove the stampede away down the lane
leaving a trail of dust and pig squeals.

On the grass slope down to the burn
we sat on cardboard boxes as sleighs
or lay sideways and barrel-rolled;
squashed snails stuck on our clothes.

Back to Granny's for diluted orange drink
and Nice biscuits. All out for soccer,
anoraks used as goalposts
until our collie dog dropped dead rats
at our feet, a present from the piggeries.

The air held the mix
of toffee sugar from the sweet factory
and the smell of pig from the empty sheds.
Oatfield's work-whistle carried on the wind.
From the bacon factory we heard death screams.

And Now I Lay Me Down To Sleep

They called it shingles,
the rash that appeared on my Mother's face
and snaked down her neck every time
my Father flew to another city on business.

I knelt at my bedside.
Look after Daddy when he is away.
Bring him safely home.

He mailed us postcards that folded out
into an accordion of pictures; Mexico,
Disneyland and Santa Barbara.

She wore an old shirt of his
to knead yeast bread that rose
like a balloon under damp dishtowels.

For dinner we had a special treat,
macaroni cheese without spuds.
One of us got to sleep in their bed.

Look after Daddy when he is away.
Always bring him safely home.

I never thought to include her.

My Mother's Birthday

I had planned for May 7th for weeks,
a surprise party and I was the only guest.
Left school at four o'clock and went straight
to the town's florist with the money
I had saved from not eating
Cola Cubes and marshmallow Snow Balls.
I walked to the end of Lower Main Street
carrying my school bag and yellow carnations,
a brown duffle coat tied around my waist by the sleeves.

I walked past a terraced row, the front door
of each home lay open and music played inside.
I walked past girls chiming skipping-rope rhymes.
I walked past the football pitch, boys under 16's
were training but I did not stop.
I walked past a man driving a tractor.
I walked past an old man with a tweed cap, his shirt
sleeves rolled up, fishing from the Swilly's bank.
I walked past a wrecked car deserted in a ditch.
I walked past a derelict home.
I walked past field after empty field
until I reached the iron graveyard gates.

It was the first birthday since she died.
There was no party.
Three sheep prowled,
chomping on the wreaths,
gnawing through the grass.
Hooves had sunk into her grave.

I brought the flowers home,
in case they trampled her gift.

February from Memory

February is the hardest month to draw back,
claw out from between all the other months.

I give you Spelling Bees in single file with flash cards,
and words like *February*, spelt wrong
that spring, bear-trap tight, to cripple confidence.

It is the hardest month to draw back, lodged
somewhere after that post-Santa buzz.

I give you Valentine cards, home-made crêpe hearts
passing through our schoolroom – and a whole display
plastering the library windows on Detroit Avenue.

It was a time of approaching sacrifice –
what are you going off this year?

A purgatory of a month
before Easter baskets, chocolate bunnies,
newly sewn outfits, shiny patent shoes and bonnets.

There must have been mid-term vacations,
years of mid-terms, but I can't smell the sense of liberation,
can't feel the school bell or the run home through the boys' yard.

We did that one recess – ran to the end of their playground
before they were let out, and Jeff Kantorek
had to escort us safely down through the thronging boys,

but that wasn't February.

I can give you – *oh no, it's snowing again* – and piles of slush,
when making a snowman has just become silly.

I can't sweat this month out through my pores,
can't give you lightning bugs or Popsicles or Camp Christopher
or even those early May masses with Mom as all the rest slept.

But still there were Valentines, all those damn Valentines
swarming around and never, ever, alighting.

No birthday parties, weddings or christenings,
just black ashes branding foreheads.

February was the hardest month,
with an enforced hibernation of the soul,
a getting ready for penance, and guilt-dark purple.

Sibling Memories

I remember our goat tied to a tea chest
in our front garden. When he chased
us he dragged the chest after him.
Lisa says that never happened.

I'll swear Anne lost a baby-tooth down
through the sofa, so she painted a picture
for the tooth fairy. She thinks that was Paul.

We sang *I am Siamese if you please.*
Why did we say *salami, salami, baloney?*
We chanted it as a skipping-rope rhyme,
but you place us jumping into Lakewood pool.

The line in 'Bohemian Rhapsody' – which one
of us used to sing, *for his one sausage tea?*
I was sure it was Lisa. She says it wasn't.

That moonlight night when Oliver Robinson
skimmed his father's speedboat across the bay,
he looked up and waved – towards me.
Now you insist it was towards you.

What about the Easter when I got scarlet fever
and no one remembered to bring me dinner.

Rutland Sound

Night on this barren island. A grass-cobbled street
with twelve stone houses, from rubbled
blood-coloured granite to holiday restoration.
All the homes, except ours, are in darkness.
Harsh light is in the distance on Burtonport pier.
There are stars, a full tide of stars, washing over us.

The end of summer, a soul-warming summer.
I stand with my husband, sons and cousins
where Mum holidayed, where her Mum once played.
We control the silence. The only noise can come from us.
Éist le fuaim na habhann agus gheobhaidh tú breac.
Listen to the sound of the river and you will get a trout.

I have never seen so many stars.
My breath has slowed to purring kitten.
I feel what will happen next:
my star shoots through the sky-dark waves.

In this wishing moment
the final lesions of a wound are healing.
I last summered here the year of her death.
I caught my first fish – a pollock; took to rowing
a rubber dinghy; barrel-rolled down mountainous sand-dunes
and leapt from the griddle-heat of the Back Strand into raw ocean.

There were no stars that summer.
There was a learning to lift my gaze from grave-deep shadows;
a learning to shield my eyes and search for the horizon;
a learning to look at the moon and feel the pull.
But stars, wild shooting stars that carried life-changing wishes –
only the innocent believed in those.

Boat Life

A memory of Daddy
in a rented row-boat
touring us around Schull harbour
until the oars grew tired.

Then his heartfelt purchase
of a boat to hold six,
grand enough for an engine.
Docked for years on our lawn.

He mended her each spring;
peeled off shrivelled skin,
applied a new paint colour,
all with the promise of an outing.

She had a longing for the ocean,
to dance with the waves,
but he launched her in a lake
for short warm-ups.

They shared a few trips,
slow floating waltzes
confined to tight circles
while wanting a sea tango.

He needed to hear breakers;
feel rocked in a cradle;
have salt tickle into his lungs;
shout above the engine's chant.

One night a storm struck.
The boat looked whole
until you stood at her side.
She was wrenched in two –

her stark steel frame lodged
between lake and land.
And now in a shallow pool
her wooden bones decay.

Wild Horses

It is said in Ceannconn – the Head of the Hound –
the Black and Tans came for my great-grandfather's horse,
a piebald horse that ate windfall apples from a child's palm,
who back-burdened their small farm, who cart-pulled
a whole clan the miles to Schull for Sunday mass.

They came for his horse as they came for all others,
with no intent of any speedy return.
Paddy Callaghan, staying gravestone silent, stared
at the horse who reared full height on his back legs,
brandished hooves more deadly than smuggled Fenian guns.

So the Black and Tans went away,
passed the family in their moonlight ransacking.
If Paddy and his piebald came wandering towards
a boreen checkpoint, the makeshift soldiers stood aside
as if he was Lord of West Cork, his family the heirs.

Has his Ceannconn nature passed through our blood,
a piebald-soul that can incite bone-crushing wildness?
Come between me and mine, and we'll see.

Valentine

I love you more than a rose can red,
more than Everest can high,
more now than the first time I said,

I love you. More than a quilt can bed
or a pillow can down. Don't ask me why.
I love you more than a rose can red.

You tender my heart, you tender my head,
mixed with a wildness that makes the geese fly,
and it's more now than the first time I said,

For always – before we knew what lay ahead.
It's more than a present can gift, for you're my
pulse's rhythm and I love you more than a rose can red.

It runs all through our lives; more than yeast can bread,
more than a house can home, more than a leg can thigh.
I feel it more now than the first time I said,

I will, and even more than the day we wed.
More than a cut can deep, a note can song, a sun can sky.
I love you more than a rose can red,
more now than the first time you said, *I love you.*

Knowing the Wizard

I'm in An Grianán theatre as primary school girls
dance their way around Oz.
I knew every breath of the movie.

Our Ohio sidewalk became the yellow-brick road
when the summer fog rolled off Lake Erie.
The Tin Man was Uncle Charlie with his cast-iron look;
What's new? Did you see the Snoo?
The song 'Lions and Tigers and Bears' made sense to me.
They crept around our house at night
waiting to pounce when I ran to the bathroom.

Once, we watched the movie in Rocky River hospital
after one of Auntie Gerrie's operations.
Dad led us up a concrete spiral of back stairs
– *no kids allowed* – just as Dorothy and the others
were creeping through the Wicked Witch's castle.

Lisa looked at her lying in the steel-framed bed
and said *Auntie Gerrie, are you tired?*
It became a family line, paraded out when we grew
too old to sing 'Kumbaya' or 'I'm a Sailor Home from Sea'.

We used to live in a tornado belt. No one warned us
how fast the wind would rise up.
A twister carried me from Cleveland to Letterkenny.

The fog rising from Lake Erie,
and now the stage-smoke from a four-foot
green-faced witch's castle, crimps my eyes.

It's not the huge 'Somewhere Over the Rainbow'
moments, but the unexpected: the way Lion holds
her tail close as a teddy bear and a flying monkey
suddenly smiles down from the stage at her mum.

These girls won't stay in Munchkin land.
They will have to follow the yellow brick
quite a while before they find that out.

I've only just earned my ruby slippers.
Where the heart lies the feet will wander.
When I click the heels together, I'm home.

Competition

Lincoln High School gym is packed.
I stand on the edge of the hall,
barefoot in my new black leotard.
I start to run down the polished floor,
pass by Mommy praying to St. Jude.
Marykay shouts, *Go Denny*.
I jump, both feet together, on the board
and spring in the air,
hands rest on the back of the wooden horse,
feet tuck in for a perfect vault.

From the side of my eye, I see the girls
who had written *Denise is a bitch*
on my autograph book.
Mid-flight, I pull away from them
and land on the red rubber mat.
Stumbling forward,
one foot falls in front of the other.

In Mourning

I blame Jackie Kennedy.
Her black suit, black gloves, nothing exposed.
Face covered by a black chiffon veil.
John-John saluting the star-spangled casket
as she stood, regal-still.

It was the only funeral I had ever seen.
We pored over the black-and-white *Life* photos.
I heard you admire her propriety.

I knew how to behave, Mum,
when the hearse suddenly died out
and your coffin had to be carried up Main Street.
It seemed right, in Kennedy terms,
to walk behind wearing a black lace mantilla.
Ladylike. First-ladylike.

But your young lady needed to cry.
Needed to mourn.
Needed to *caoin*.
Needed to kneel down in the mud
and howl like an orphaned cub.

Metronome

This triangle of sheen-polished mahogany,
not quite a toy, but a gift nevertheless.
Piano lessons with my Godmother aunt
at her Baby Grand on Rocky River Avenue.
The clocklike swing. The tick-tocking
sound braiding through all the crotchets
I would take from the page and strike.

She wanted to infuse that tempo into me,
teach me the even-measured tone,
restraint, ladylike poise and composure.
A tick-tock balance of quavers in perfect pitch.
She stayed as serene as that slow pulse beat
while I hit the bum notes, and she never flinched
when my chords became a string of flat stresses.

The sound smoothed my imperfect symphony
and the sound soothed her imperfect harmony.
And when I left her to return to our kid-filled zone
on Bonnieview Avenue, did this sparrow-light
woman still play to that sedating rhythm?
Metron nomos, metron nomos, metron nomos,
clocking away the silence of her childless home.

Early Lessons

Aunt Mary wanted to mould me into a lady,
little finger cocked when drinking from a china cup.
She soaked me in classical music,
brought me in her Cadillac through the ghetto
to the Greater Cleveland Art Gallery.
When I needed to visit the Ladies, she lined
the seat with long strips of paper tissue.

Years later, I return to the States.
Browse in a mall, queue to use the toilets.
The cubicle door opens. A tall woman steps out –
my age, my height, but not my colour.
I feel Aunt Mary near me, feel Aunt Mary in me.
As if the door had just swung into my face,
I realise why she reached for reams of white tissue.

And I'm back in her library,
cocooned in a winged leather chair
reading *How Green Was My Valley*.
I hear a wash of conversation, the adults:
property prices will fall if just one family
of them move in. We'd be overrun.

I remember the bullet of shock
going through me, my school, my town,
when Bobby Kennedy was killed,
instead of the slight sting as if grazed
by a peashooter, for Martin Luther King.
What quagmire am I rooted in?

Grave Distance

As kids we became unglued from each other;
stuck to the far walls or different floors,
corners of our bedrooms or just sofa edges.

Shouting distance was good:
Someone take the clothes off the line.

Nodding distance was all right:
When did you get your hair cut?

Even skirting past,
as long as we kept skirting past:
I'll get the messages after school.

Arm's length if need be:
Did you see the match of this sock?

But never near enough to feel breath;
never break-down-on-shoulder close,
never look into my eyes, watch me drown.

Remnants

I found a case in the attic
three years after Mummy died.
Blue and green tartan vinyl
hoarding her dressmaking ends.

I held each piece to find
the trace of Tweed perfume:
a tomato-shaped pin cushion
worn wrapped around her wrist
as she tacked us together;
the measuring tape used to decree
how mini was my miniskirt;
velvet ribbons that tied our Easter bonnets.

There were scraps from outfits she had made:
marshmallow-pink cotton with white polka dots
for 'Singing in the Rain' at the school concert;
broderie anglaise, my sister's communion dress;
navy jersey of a baby boy's sailor suit;
lime-green bouclé that made Mummy
Jackie Kennedy chic;
psychedelic red and blue prints
for my first bell-bottom pants;
gold satin of her ball gown.

I saw those swathes of fabrics
she had folded for our future.
Closing the case was pulling down
the coffin lid again.

We had our proms, our weddings,
our babies' christenings,
dressed in store-bought clothes.

The Splice

We are here, wrapped by the Atlantic
on Rutland, the island of my mother's people.
These pink-drizzled granite walls housed
a whole Rosses-bred line of my being.

They are here with me, head to head, my father
and my eleven-year-old son, working over strands
they have pulled out of a rope, braiding –
a sea-blooded man teaching a land-born boy.

I've never watched their features so closely,
two profiles intent on the criss-cross of cord.
Island air has teased the grey and the blond
into tight fishermen's curls.

In this light, as rain washes the far-off landscape
out of the picture, I see the same taper of jaw,
the same line of their nose, and yet my son's gaze
comes through my mother's brown eyes.

A loop is beginning to work back on itself
while youth takes the rope from weather-worn
hands and holds a third strand in his pale palm.
He is mastering the weave.

Boatmen know this. You can drop this loop
over a post and a boat will hold fast to the pier.
My son is learning; tight knots, clan knots,
turning tides and when to cut a boat into a wave.

For as long as we stay on my mother's island,
through days when winds could shear the grass
off the land; for as long as he keeps returning,
he will need my father's knowledge for survival.

The rope-end has formed into a strong circle
between the experience and the learning.
My father holds the cord as his grandson
pulls their work with all his strength.

The loop keeps. The rope is secure.
Strong enough to hold a boat to shore.
Between them the splice is complete.

Vows

I, Donna Maria Rochester Hurley, take thee, Paddy Boyle
as my third husband. My love eternal. My final choice
so long as you accept:
my two daughters, Maria and Juanita, from my first marriage
to Juan Aquia Estibia and the regular visits of his two sons,
Jesus and Manolo to his first wife Antonia (who is not well),
but we won't be bothered by his son Rodrigo
by his second wife (who was a bitch), Phillipa.
I share joint custody of my two sons, Tod and Jeff,
by my second husband, Joey Pastromi. I see them every
second Sunday in the winter months and the first two weeks
of each summer month. They spend one Christmas with me,
the next with their Father, and the third one with Joey's children
Becky and Beth in the winter home of his second wife
Kelly Anne (who was independently wealthy
and did not need any alimony from Joey).

For richer or poorer, in sickness and in health, till death do us part.

I, Paddy Boyle, take thee, Donna Maria Rochester Hurley
to be my wife, so long as you understand:
my aged mother, Margaret Magdeline will have to live with us.
She'll never be a bother, only give you a bit of advice since
you're a blow-in. We'll have the occasional visit from my sister,
Maggie and her four children but not from that useless
man she married (he never did a day's work). We'll help her
out the odd time; for school uniforms, Christmas, Birthdays,
Communions, Confirmations and the wee trip away for her nerves.
We'll see my brother John when he gets kicked out
of his home because his lazy wife doesn't understand
a man needs a few pints to get through a day.
And then there is our Jimmy. He is still looking for a lassie
who is a good housekeeper. Until he does, you'll just feed
him lunch and a decent dinner. Potatoes and meat.
None of your pasta nonsense. We'll probably have my uncles,
aunts and cousins drop in for a cuppa every Mart day, Dole day,
after evening mass, Stations and Graveyard Sunday.

For richer or poorer, in sickness and in health, till death do us part.

Rathlin Island

Five hundred left in one day,
stepped from this small island
onto a waiting coffin ship
after the fungus seeped
through potato starch,
spreading the stench of death.

Wind over the waves raises steam
like breath on a cold window-pane.
The cliffs are ridged from fingernails
clawed down the black earth
as their thoughts tried to climb home.
White dust on the shore is their ashes.

Out in the water, a rock
has worn down into a giant foot
taking its first step away;
in its centre is a stake,
a crucifixion,
holding it to Rathlin.

Long Dresses

You are the wearing of a new dress,
not just a new dress, but an evening gown.
You are the fancy frock I never want to take off –
like those girls the morning after Trinity Ball,
flouncing through the streets of Dublin.

I felt it first in '73 when I borrowed
Joan O'Donnell's maxi for the folk festival dance.
I lived in her dress all that night – daisy-patterned
calico with anglaise frills on the collar and sleeves –
pincering the ends of the skirt to glide down our lino stairs,
over and over, when I wasn't swizzing with the coat stand.

I borrowed Mairead's pure-white Edwardian chiffon
for that Cathal Brugha Street dinner dance.
The night before, I practised in her dress,
solo-waltzing up St. Mary's hostel corridors, swishing
though cubicle curtains and around St. Martin de Porres.

The finest was my wedding dress;
lace top with a mandarin collar, pearl buttons,
fluted sleeves, chiffon with layers of petticoats, a train
with a loop on the skirt to wrap around my wrist if I danced.
I did dance. My hem kissed every inch of the maple floor.
The dress was mine. More than that, you were mine.

A woman once said, *the best thrill is going to buy new shoes
while wearing new shoes* – but for me
it's a gown that gives me beautiful.
You give me an *I-want-this-to-last-forever* feeling.
With you, I could dance all night.

Annual Storage

Once again, Ian, we dismantle Santa.
Unplugged, his warm body goes cold,
but for you he has already been dismantled.

You lost him somewhere between last year's
hoarding away and last month's resurrection from the attic.

Restore in December, re-stow under the rafters in January.
Every crystal bauble, statued Madonna, swaddled infant,
will soon be bubble-wrapped or styrofoamed.

Already our new year begins to unreel. Come next winter
what dove of feelings will be released with the decorations?

Last Christmas among the Lego pieces and wrestling figures
you found a new guitar; and this year you can play
a perfect version of Bob Marley's 'Redemption Song'.

Today is called Women's Christmas. I encase
two drummer-boys: tokens engraved for your older brothers
when they used to search for Santa's footprints in the ashes.

Now their thoughts are on presents for girlfriends and presents
from girlfriends and *Who's the Boxing Night D.J. in the Grill?*

The boxes are sealed. The attic ladder is unfolded.
There is a trail of dry pine needles heading out the door.

Happy Christmas (War Is Over)

I once knew Christmas. I could have lit up
the city of Cleveland with my pulsating belief.

I skated in Rockefeller Centre, all red skates
and panda-coated warmth, as I iced past the tallest
tree, gliding clockwise, with my Mother waving
at my every rotation, every scramble for balance.

I knew Christmas when Paulo first discovered it
as he mountain-crawled through our presents –
Dad in the corner cine-filming while Lisa's
walking doll rebounded off the legs of the dining-table.

And all the times that Santa had mislabelled the wrapping,
so Mom re-jiggled the parcels; right up to our first Irish
Nollaig with uncles, aunts, cousins all bunged into Granny's.
So this is Christmas, the near and the dear ones,

So this is Christmas, the world is so wrong,
Lennon's song on the radio, when even Santa's visit
could not redress our family's December loss.
I still know Christmas, I just don't trust it.

Mountain Moods

The mountain changes colour with her moods,
he tells me as I step over a mid-floor hoover.
I hear the screech of newspapers shining a window.

The base of Maumlack is coffee-bean brown
sprinkled with lady's smock lilac.
The mountain lightens into a spring-meadow green.

His wife enters the room peeling off Marigold gloves,
hands flailing to excuse the house's state,
but the weans are all coming home for Easter.

They insist I have tea from a cosied pot,
plates of range-baked scones, gingered rhubarb jam.
I steal from the hoard made for their brood.

Sunlight throws off the granite like a camera's flash.
The mountain preens into postcard shades;
heather, buttercup and mineral-bubbled springs.

Grandchildren will shake the house.
The women will watch their brother's girlfriend –
hold her like a pure crystal vase, searching for flaws.

Rooms accordion out into every corner.
Roast duck spits in the pan, sounds are stewed,
stories diverge through a forest of asides.

The heart of Maumlack purrs like a hearthside tabby,
turns from embered garnet to hot-whiskey amber.
Clouds blanket in pillowed cotton wool.

Monday. The home deflates into an empty husk.
Flesh-warm beds are stripped bare,
skull-white china entombed.

The body of the mountain turns raven-black.
Creeping thistle veins into winter-capped grey.
The air becomes too tight to breathe.

Sleep Watch

And still you sleep.
Two ceiling lights shine like stars
through orange chiffon.
The room smells of Lysol,
floor polish and Lynx body spray.
I hear a buzzer ringing.

Pain has been sedated.
The red fever flush has lifted.
Pink foam cubes on lollipop sticks
soak in a kidney dish
to wet your parched lips.

And still you sleep.
A monster radio and stack of CDs
take over the steel-grey locker;
computer magazines on the window-sills.
Basketball boots, size ten, peek out
from under the straight-backed chair.

You are the length of the bed,
one arm sweeping the floor.
A day's growth turning
to a ginger-tinged stubble.
Your hair teasing into tiny curls.

I watched you sleep before
in a room just like this,
swaddled by a boy-blue wrap,
in a cot with glass sides
clear as Cinderella's slipper.

Breathe

Mum used to say, *Take a deep breath*
when we reached the point of our Sunday drive:
Lough Salt; Magheraroarty; Ards Forest Park.

A returned emigrant who needed to breathe in
the whole of our county, purify her city-clogged
soul. Home colour returning to her cheeks.

I took a breath yesterday when that letter arrived
for Miss McGlinchey. The *Miss* dragging me back
way before my childhood. Mum's communion half-crown

has now reached final savings. There has been interest
labouring all this time, labouring thirty years past
her time: *and we do not appear to have received a reply.*

I Sunday-drove to Dunlewy today. A sorrow-cold
air held all of the valley in one eternal state.
Clouded heavens reflected in the lake's Madonna blue
as the pulsing wind whispered *Take a deep breath.*

On Reading *One Art* by Elizabeth Bishop

Reels of cine film holding us as kids
disintegrate in boxes under the stairs.
In the attic a rust-hinged trunk
contains the remains of sewing patterns,
your black patent pocket-book, flour-dusted
apron and chiffon scarf smelling of Oil of Olay.

I've encased your yellowed letters
in our home's cornerstone,
lined the wall's cavity with old photographs,
sealed mementos in the chimney pots,
souvenirs in the eaves.

I sunk Rocky River Drive in our foundations,
nailed Lakewood under the floorboards,
and bricked Ohio in behind my wardrobe.

I did not lose all our memories, Mum,
I buried them in my chest freezer, below popsicles,
chuck burgers and frosted birthday cakes.

The Haunting

This country hotel room has a glass-eyed chill.
Blue-budded wallpaper is sucking the fragrance
out of my soul. I can feel voices rising
from the night-shadowed carpet.
Bone-white curtains lift and fall in a last gasp.
I taste the grief of a stranger's funeral,
but I must find sleep this weary night.

Outside, in the field once tilled for landlords,
a horse, unicorn-white, stands alabaster-still,
evoking some memory of Sir Lancelot.
If I remain in his clay-rooted vision
I will be safe. His presence parts the tear-damp pall.
There are more things in heaven and earth, Horatio,
Than are dreamt of in your philosophy.

The weary ghosts of Mayo can't haunt me.
I have seen grief in flesh and bone
and I haunt my own ghosts nightly,
rattle marbled rosary beads of memories,
reading from my spine-cracked diary.
The phantoms of someone else's pain
will never shake my nerves in fear.

I chant, *you really don't want to be bothering me*
until the room soothes its afterlife lodgers.
The odour changes to babies' breath.
Primroses blossom on the starched curtains.
I am left alone carrying my own ghosts.
But still, under the droop of the linen pelmet
is the steady gaze from Camelot's horse.

Fishing Time

1

I always knew this black-and-white photograph would exist –
three boys standing in a bath-sized boat that is tied pier-side.
They are holding up thin cord lines weighted by hooks.
You're at the end in wash-faded clothes, all floppy-haired and smiling.

What age are you there? Ten, eleven? By sixteen you were inland
at a counter job. How much did it hurt to move from Schull?
The solid ground scourged your feet, weakened your leg muscles,
and the air, in that northern place, hadn't any sea salt, only dry dust.

On our family holidays instinct led us climbing into tied boats
to reach the furthest one, any old board, so long as we could travel.
A shoal of silver-bellied mackerel sprung from the harbour's waters
as we strained to row farther than the fraying rope would let us go.

For you, the rope has always been straining.
All those years when your own boat lay landlocked on our lawn,
all those years when grandchildren leapt into imaginary oceans
until that old boat became so bone dry it would have drowned.

2

Why do we travel this far just for the sicknesses and the deaths?
It is only here that we can stand graveside as soul-pure sails
float towards melting amber; only here will the tides turn from tear-blue
to kingfisher-blue, and the air brings out the freckles of your youth.

While we sort through the remnants of your brother's life,
the sea has calmed to heartbeat-still. I hear the waves whisper.
Down by barnacled rocks a seal watches with the eyes of Father Time.
I feel all this in my earth-clogged veins. What of your ocean blood?

You can stay indoors and small talk through responsibilities
but by the morning Fastnet Rock will be far from your back again.
The last of those three boys needs to climb into a pier-side boat.
Go fishing Dad, cast it all away for a light line and a hook-sized weight.

Ever This Day Be at My Side

My mother is the Scarlett O'Hara of heaven,
trying to take care of all of my tomorrows.
She was a Saturday night sherry and a Crunchie;
the teddy softness of a black fur jacket;
a dinner tray to my flu-bed;
dancing in our kitchen to Greek music
and Robert Goulet's blue eyes.

I can keep my sons safe as eggshells.
If I hold them too close, they will be crushed.
I'm sure they will scour out their own trouble,
for they didn't lick that off the ground.

Yet, the light from my childhood fireworks
still burns as the Arlington grave's flame.
Our railway line really was a safe place to play
and I never did fall out of a tree.

So I'll watch them from the nearest redwood,
blowing dandelion seeds of grace.
When I'm gone they'll feel the sound
of poetry books closing,
and *Carrickfergus* sung slightly off-kilter.
They won't know me, but they'll know me.
A mháthair i gcónaí, their very own guardian angel.

Sounding the Time

Wedged in the crenellation of a castle's battlement
waiting for the one o'clock cannon to sound.
Bob and I are touristing in Edinburgh
while Aiden freshers in his university nearby.

This morning we trekked the Museum of Childhood,
as Bob's childhood years fizzle away; soon
he won't walk on the same side of the road as me.
Filing past shelved memorabilia I kept saying, *I remember.*

I remember that brand of sherbet fizz ricocheted in my mouth,
how those skipping-rope rhymes called the initials of a future
boyfriend, and pulling Sindy's hair longer out a hole in her head.
I remember my teens within breathing distance.

Glass-cased exhibits kaleidoscoped with memories;
teething rings I gave to my babies, *The Cat in the Hat,*
fringed cowboy breeches, the Ghost-Buster backpacks.
Their early morning scramble to watch *Wacaday.*

We came to one doll with a long-dead pallor,
like Bette Davis in *Whatever Happened to Baby Jane,*
wearing Miss Havisham's wedding dress. Encased.
Horrored from being stuck in the past.

Bob leans forward on the castle wall as a red-coated
guard solo-marches towards the roped-off field gun.
The city that Aiden already calls home, petticoats out from us
and one misheard line from a song keeps ear-worming me –

it's crazy, being twenty-two, feeling seventeen.
Boom. It is one o'clock.
One o'clock, February 19th, 2004.
There is no mistaking the sound of the present.

Landing on the Moon

The moon mission marks the difference.
Pre-landing was fifth grade in Lincoln School.
We were caught in a Cape Kennedy carnival –
all science projects with solar systems.

Then we emigrated to Donegal, or re-emigrated,
or just moved home – June '69 and our focus altered
like the psychedelic shapes of a kaleidoscope.

Everyone I knew in Ohio watched Apollo 11.
The Fratoes would have sat up late, ordered out pizza,
drank quarts of Pepsi (they weren't a Coca-Cola house).

We had moved five hours away – a whole mind-switch.
I've no memory of even watching mankind's giant
first steps on the black-and-white telly in Granny's.

And yet I can picture our TV in '63 after the assassination,
men in suits and hats leading Oswald down a corridor,
Ruby with the gun followed by Oswald's grimace.

I learned the dark and light shades of the moon story,
the wrongs and rights of the grassy knoll story,
while I orbited from Irish-American to American-Irish.

What was real was lightning bugs dancing through the sky
as we ate buttered popcorn on Fratoes' front porch,
and that summer's shift to tuppenny sweets after twenty-a-side
rounders on real Irish fields. What else was real no longer matters.

In the Final Innings

There are still times when a word, a sound, a smell
collides with my senses in a pile-up with memory.
I carry a baseball bat for these moments,
take the whole ball of grief and try to wallop it away;
away from my home, away from this town, away
across the ocean and through the rain clouds.

And my field becomes cleared of dark emotions
until another collision occurs:
a stranger asks, *Are you Eileen's daughter?*,
Engelbert Humperdinck re-releases her favourite song,
parenting becomes so hard I need to be mothered.
All the feelings boomerang back.

I want the needles of loss to whir on past me.
I want to smell Elnett hairspray, see Jackie Kennedy
sunglasses or taste butter melted on home-baked bread
and have it feel simple, as harmless as a cup of milk.
Not this hangover that rattles through my nerves.
I want to finally let my batting arm lie at rest.

Sea Hand

It drags me to the shore of Rutland Island.
A hand thrusts into the ice-cold ocean
of my wintered moments,
into water that changes from the marine blue
of my grandmother's eyes to the raw umber
of stagnant, untouched memories.

This hand swims like an eel through the waves
of all my life; the inner curl of a baby asleep
in her mother's arms, the white-ridged froth
of Christmas mornings, the wild crashing down
of a sudden loss and the unexpected lift,
wind blowing a squall towards the east.

A hand crusted with layers of sea salt,
coated through generation after generation,
reaches inland to tap me on the shoulder.
Spins me around to face my other shore,
lets fall the final grains from the Back Strand
trailing in a path to lead me home.

The Birthday Concert

I fought with Cliona
the morning of my fifth birthday.
We held a strained truce as all our cousins
sat around the red tartan car rug
laid out on Granny's yard.

After sponge cake and minerals
the adults called for a concert.
A sheet was tied from the gooseberry bush
to the outside toilet door.
We prepared our party pieces.

The curtain raised for the first performer,
our second cousin Maureen from Dublin.
She sang a song with a full open mouth,
arms thrown out, a copycat Shirley Temple.
All the adults clapped.

Maureen spun around
and danced a jig
as far as the piggery and back
in her feis-winning routine.
The adults were thrilled.

There was the curtain,
and there was Maureen
reciting a poem with clear,
crisp brown-cow sounds.
The adults were in tears.

Cliona came across the blanket
and sat beside me.
First cousins.

Ever Blooming

I remember the cherry blossoms from that visit.
Out of our express bus, the Finglas Road flowed past
in a carnival of springtime colour.
The Easter before my Leaving cert
and those trees smelt of future promise,
sang of my past until it was finally over.
I wanted to garland the flowers in my hair,
I wanted to brooch them to my heart.

Now I remember not only the cherry blossoms,
but the fertile fruit lolling around Henry Street stalls,
the spiced saris floating through Dandelion Market,
and the love-locked couples lying on Stephen's Green.
What's for you won't go by you – I knew that,
but I wanted to lasso the whole city
in case it wasn't for me; for fear my possibilities
would leap onto the horse-drawn carts and ride off.

Dublin's jammering noise gave me peace, soothed me.
I dived into the Liffey to wash myself clean,
as my memories floated away in the oil-slurped bubbles.
I will go back again, before my winter takes root
and catch the cherry blossoms as they turn to confetti.
An rud a líonas an tsúil líonann sé an croí –
What fills the eye fills the heart – that spring
the city clasped me in her arms and mothered me.

Old Man in a Barber's Chair

In this photo, an old man and a youth are vivid
while their background fades into sepia.
His face is as my grandmother's in her final days
with that smile she held, believing she was sixteen.

Traffic passes outside their window.
There is a passing also in the snip-snip of scissors,
youth cutting away the grey
while the dusk-lit middle-aged wait.

A host of sunlight rests on the old man
like a dove poised on his finger,
ready to move from the elder to the youth.
For the gift moves on from each generation.

And this is how it was for us,
this passing on of knowledge;
how to bake scones, cheat at poker,
how to be eighty-four and sixteen all at once.

Her gift now rests in my hands;
light and dark reflected and crystalised.
I will pass it on as the negative fades,
before the scissors make their final cut.

Theme Tune

The singer says he has the lyrics first,
may be ten years until he has the music,
ten years until he has a song.

I could hear our theme as an Ohio child.
Makem and Clancy tunes ran through everything –
fourth of July picnics to 'When Irish Eyes Are Smiling'.

Then the record handle started scraping
back and forth as on a warped LP.
If only there had been a song played in warning –
'Somewhere Over the Rainbow',
or the whole soundtrack of *Camelot*.
We were living through endings –
last Christmas, last birthday, last Mother's Day.

But life doesn't come with a soundtrack.
So this Sunday dinner (as we fight over
the turning off or keeping on of the Simpsons)
might be accompanied by *misty water-coloured memories*,
if we could only hear.

It's not the same to re-run an old family video
and add a theme tune.

I've years of words and years of music.
I'm still working on the song.

And They Say Time Is Like a River

The Athi River in Kenya doesn't flow all year,
but Masai herdsmen marshal their cattle
for miles to reach the scorched earth
where wave patterns ripple in sand.
Cows stretch parched tongues into saucered
puddles, shower themselves in dust.
Flesh recedes from bone while vultures circle.

The Cuyahoga River in Ohio went on fire.
Oil-sodden water blazed
for days in barbecued humidity.
The fourth of July fireworks partied
as flames danced towards Lake Erie.
Leisure-boats fled for their lives
while firemen fought to put out the river.

In Irish waters the fish of knowledge
battle through brown-speckled rivers
towards their remembered birthplace.
Leap high-rise to hurdle into a stream
that is gone; steel-shuttered away.
Leap and leap until their remains
are washed back into the watershed.

A Note for My Hosts

I left a few buns in a Mace bag
on your farmhouse kitchen table.
They are in the corner
between the sugar-dusted apple-pie
and the floral bowl full of radishes.
I want you to know I brought them as a swap
for all I eat as we snug in at your poets' supper.
The buns are freshly baked, but not by me,
and that is where I break a cycle.

Within this place – in the seagulls' chants,
the seaweed smell in the air, the tweed
of the landscape and the trawler etching
across the horizon – are all the women
whose lives spanned into mine.

Apron-clad women with purple-stained
fingers from their berry bushes,
who used eggs warm from under the hen,
milk with a froth like sea spray
and butter with the sheen of buttercups.
All mixed with the strength of their hand,
cakes, wholemeal scones and puddings
placed on a big farmhouse kitchen table.

Next time when I'm invited to your home
I'll bring some buns, home-baked.

Muckish Road

Where earth turns from birch-cane brown
to worn-saddle tan, and granite turns from knuckle white
to parched bone. Pebbles grow from both sides of the road
up into sheer chiffon cloud. Stone forms into a mountain,
eclipsing the light. Demanding silence.

The crush of tyres on tarmac is loud voices in a cathedral.
Shush the radio. Genuflect and kneel down,
kneel down and let the valley echo an invocation.

Let those who have passed come out from the quarry:
those with a suitcase and a one-way ticket to America;
those with a bundle of clothes heading to the hiring;
those with nothing but the fare for a coffin ship;
those fleeing from feudal lords and tribal chiefs,
let them all appear, for they are here.

To Isaac Rosenberg

Do Isaac Rosenberg, Cathal Ó Searcaigh
translation, Denise Blake

The light is dawn as we stroll home
from our courting in the wooded wilderness.
Larks rise from the holes and hollows of Prochlais.

With that, I think of you, Isaac Rosenberg,
war-worn on the overthrown fields of France.
You were listening to the dawn song of the larks

while returning to your camp. Returning over the broken
bones of your friends, as the harrowing staccato
of bursting bombs turned the battled darkness crimson.

I hear the spirit of the larks between the air and water,
and your poems appear to me in the no-man's land of eternity,
line by line; faltering, fearful as soldiers at the mouth of slaughter.

The words humble me in their exposition of such horror:
the black holes of the trenches; doomed dreams of young boys;
massacres. They loom in the shadows of my uneasy conscience –

this man who has never been in the breach of bloodshed,
never attempted a fatal charge over the top into destruction,
or never once had to endure a gory, heart-stopping defeat.

I never saw fresh-faced soldiers thrown like straw sheaths
in the fertile fields of warfare; smelt a deathly stench
rising as a plague from the rotting flower of youth;

never wore the carnage-soaked muck of a battleground;
lost my mind in the sound of explosions; nor felt the hot sting
of a bullet, like a wasp sucking out the wild honey of my life.

No, don't be offended, Isaac Rosenberg, by my using your name,
I who am shielded by my poems in this sanctuary of love
while the red wound of war still festers in the heart of Europe.

For my soul was joyous from the closeness of that wonderful body.
My lover at my side; each limb, each muscle, each promontory,
each portion of him from his crown to the ground – all so enticing.

I believe now, when we are entwined in each other's arms
there is a protection from danger. Life is full of generosity.
The song of our love is our safety from every dissension.

The larks sing to me what they used to sing to you
before you were blown to the heavens –
companionship and music surpass rivalry and conflict.

Although I have never been in the jaws of combat,
and I have only ever frittered away my paltry lifetime
hibernating from current events in my cloistered corner,

I would like to assure you, beloved poet, who was unwavering
with your words, who spoke the stark truth amid the slaughter –
I am with you on the side of Light, with you on the side of Life.